THE INTERNAL SABOTEUR

MUSAWENKOSI KHANYILE

This is a work of fiction. All names, characters, places, and incidents are a product of the author's imagination. Any resemblance to real events or persons, living or dead, is entirely coincidental.

Published by Akashic Books

ISBN: 978-1-61775-746-4

Printed in China
First printing

Akashic Books
Brooklyn, New York, USA
Ballydehob, Co. Cork, Ireland
Twitter: @AkashicBooks
Facebook: AkashicBooks
E-mail: info@akashicbooks.com
Website: www.akashicbooks.com

African Poetry Book Fund
Prairie Schooner
University of Nebraska
110 Andrews Hall
Lincoln, Nebraska 68588

TABLE OF CONTENTS

PREFACE
by Len Verwey

Musawenkosi Khanyile is a South African poet who works as a clinical psychologist. He was born and raised in Nseleni Township, close to the Eastern coastline of the continent.

He is a young, exciting voice in South African poetry. His poems have appeared in various journals over the last few years, but this chapbook is a first chance to see a group of them together.

One is struck firstly by the everyday language, the accessibility of these poems.

There is little that is overtly and pretentiously "poetic" about them, and yet they carry nuances of meaning, move powerfully and poignantly between the past and the present, and find a lovely, constantly shifting balance of sadness, humour, desire, and anger that makes them a real poetry gift.

They present a man who is the product of a mother who left early and a father who did his best, but was constrained by his own maleness and the limits put on him by apartheid.

A writing, thinking, adult man who wants to love and be loved, but who cannot help but sabotage the matter, cannot help but turn away from the lover and from intimacy.

In the first, title poem, we are introduced to the father and the son, living wifeless and motherless. We get strong line after strong line: "our hearts never came out of our rooms," for example. The only conversation between them happens while watching soccer on TV, when, one infers, they have a shared, neutral topic to talk about.

But again, in the car drives both father and son can only listen to the humming of the engine. And again appears the lingering image of the boy who learns

to store his voice within [him] for the silent days

like ants store food ahead of winter.

Turning to the mother, who left with the younger siblings, we find already in this first poem the hard honesty and the deep ambivalence that the speaker brings to bear on his relationship with her:

> I swung back and forth
> from loving to hating to tolerating her.
> A part of me was happy when she left.
> Now she calls to complain that I never call.

Along with a more subtle, sinister game of power between a mother and a son, we sense in the coming forwards and the stepping back, that this is a larger game that the characters are doomed to play with future lovers:

> You are worried that you left
> even where you should have stayed.
> We have a strange relationship;
> we starve of each other for months,
> and when you can no longer bear it,
> you call for what seems like reassurance.

This is all heavy stuff, but there is also, from the start, a wry, delicious humour that runs through many of the poems, lightly carried, perfectly timed. Before the mother and the father are introduced, for example, the grade 8 boy's hand lands on the "delicate parts of a classmate"; one teacher suggests, as a remedy, that the boy cut down on cheese.

In the "Mother" poems, "Absence" begins with a boy's deluded sense of the value of "women's work" versus "men's work," conveyed with admirable succinctness. For the boy, thinking of his mother: "you only buttered bread, never bought it."

As such, she hardly worked, the boy thinks. But, with her gone, it turns out that men do not cope so well with the quotidian, the need to maintain the everyday by just doing what needs to be done:

> The house here is falling apart.
> Even the kitchen door handle broke.
> Dad put in five nails on the side
> to keep it locked at night.
> I throw a used teabag through a broken window
> by the kitchen sink
> where the air comes smashing
> against the curtain on windy days.

Hinted here is the suggestion that more than the house is falling apart. But, apart from offering a more than decent metaphor, what Musa Khany- ile brings that is especially his is the concrete detail, as in the five nails on the side, as in the teabag thrown through the broken window.

In "The sound of the rain," the literal problem of a neglected and hence now leaking house is rendered in the beautiful line: "in this house the rain doesn't quit on the rooftop." And here we also see Khanyile's skill for bring- ing in the heavy matters of politics and history without resorting to rheto- ric or empty proclamations. Again, the precise image does the work; aside from this being a motherless house, it is the house of a man and father who could not prosper though he worked all his life, because he could not get the better jobs reserved for whites:

> a job that has still not rescued us
> from leaking roofs,
> even though your long-service certificates are fading inside the wall unit.

The last poem of the "Father" series is a tribute, and it is meaningful because it carries in it the knowledge of the father's weaknesses as well as his strengths. The speaker enjoins himself to unlearn his father's temper, to unlearn his silence, but knows that what he should take with him is his father's humility, his smile, and above all, his love and his strength:

> I must put all my failed relationships to shame,
> and learn to love like you do—
> learn to love until photos look centuries old.
> I should pray for the strength you carried us with.
> I should pray.

These then are the templates for the relationships that are explored in the final "Lovers" section. "First girl visit: High School" is such a complex blend of themes of young love, bittersweet humour, and underlying economic realities.

A relentless, unwavering honesty informs all the poems in the "Lovers" section. Though there is tenderness, what drives the speaker is the fear that he cannot get away: that what we carry from our childhood and youth, what we had to do to get through, shapes our intimate relations forever.

The coldness directed at the mother who left, for example, plays out again in the cruel treatment of the lover in "One of the ways in which we ended," who comes from some distance to be with him, and who he turns away callously with an obvious lie.

In the final poem of the collection, the speaker questions the very possibility that our hearts could be an abiding place for others, too:

> My heart is a hotel room up the stairs.
> Lovers are always walking up and down
> looking for a home.

It is a measure of the strength of the writing that, at the end, one is invested, taken. One hopes, with the speaker, that there's a way for him, and for us, to enter into adult connection.

For mom and dad and all those who came and went.

THE INTERNAL SABOTEUR

In grade 8, my hand landed on the delicate parts of a classmate.
This did not look anything like me:
a well-behaved boy who always wore neatly
and performed well in class.
She reported me.
One teacher said I needed to cut down on cheese.

Back home there was only my father—
a man who lived within himself.
We turned the house into separate homes;
our hearts never came out of our rooms.
We met briefly on our coincidental walks to the kitchen.
Also in the lounge when soccer was playing on TV.
That is the only time we ever spoke.
Even when we drove a distance
we listened to the humming of the engine.
I learned to store his voice within me for the silent days
like ants store food ahead of winter.

Mom had gone to live in a rural area,
in a house that dad built on the conviction that men
should retire away from the restlessness of the township.
She'd taken my younger siblings with her.
I was in primary school.

Mom raised me with a loud voice and a short temper.
I remember her pressing me against the ground,
hitting me with all the energy she possessed.
I swung back and forth

from loving to hating to tolerating her.
A part of me was happy when she left.
Now she calls to complain that I never call.

I grew up in solitude.
Learned to enjoy silence.
Got used to keeping myself to myself.
Found poetry in high school and hid myself there.

Girls came and went.
Relationships slipped through my hands.
Maybe because I never learned to share myself.
Maybe because of mom and dad and silence.
The psychologist in Hilton asked me:
who then taught you affection?
and then scribbled down a note when I couldn't answer.
That was the last time I saw her.

MOTHER

MOTHER

Dad built a house in a rural area.
He didn't want to die in the township;
he thought his soul wouldn't find peace
in such an unsettled place.
You left to stay in this house.
I was in primary school.

Now many years have passed.
You are worried that you left
even where you should have stayed.
We have a strange relationship;
we starve of each other for months,
and when you can no longer bear it,
you call for what seems like reassurance.
My heart feels heavy inside my chest
when after months
you call to ask if I still love you.

ABSENCE

You used to say what we have
is because of you.
I did not understand
because you never worked
anywhere else but in the house.
You only buttered bread, never bought it.
But now that you live away from us,
I see what you meant.
The house here is falling apart.
Even the kitchen door handle broke.
Dad put in five nails on the side
to keep it locked at night.
I throw a used teabag through a broken window
by the kitchen sink
where the air comes smashing
against the curtain on windy days.
None of this has moved dad yet.
He still walks in with his dirty sandals
all the way to his bedroom.
I place a bucket there when it rains.
Holes in roofs beckon one another
like shacks do outside the township.
There used to be a single hole there,
now there are three,
so I push the bed to the far right
for the drops to miss it,
and place another bucket in the middle of the room.
There's more than the falling apart
going on here.
Even the curtains miss your touch.
Their dullness whispers this to me.

ABSOLUTION

I should have known that I could never run away from you.
You visit me now in the guise of a lover.
In her beautiful eyes I see you;
through her soft touch, I'm forgiving you.

FATHER

YOUR LOVE

Your love was like road signs.
I only read your face to understand
when to stop
where to go.
We did not need a voice to love;
love was quiet and enough.
Things have changed:
now you want to speak more
like a man desperate to leave something behind
before he goes.
Your thirst for conversation
draws you out of your room.
Sometimes I want to shut you out
even if it hurts.
Sometimes I want to avenge
all the silent years.

THE SOUND OF THE RAIN

The sound of the rain wakes me up in the middle of the night.
Or is it the noise coming from your room,
your bed squeaking and raindrops hitting against the basin?
You have moved your bed such that it now stands misaligned with the
    headboard.
The mop rests next to where you've been busy drying up after the rain.
In this house the rain doesn't quit on the rooftop.
It lands on the bed, and then after someone's labour, finds the basin.
You are here tonight, so it is your turn to move your bed.
My turn is when you are away on a job that has still not rescued us from
    leaking roofs,
even though your long-service certificates are fading inside the wall unit.

I SHOULD PRAY

I must unlearn your temper.
I must unlearn your silence.
I should take your humility and cut myself a half.
Take your smile. Give it freedom to come out more
often. And wear it.
I must put all my failed relationships to shame,
and learn to love like you do—
learn to love until photos look centuries old.
I should pray for the strength you carried us with.
I should pray.

LOVER

IN THE BEGINNING

In the beginning there was a mother who loved me the best way she knew how.

In the beginning there was a father who loved me the best way he knew how.

The mother only knew to love with a loud voice.

The father only knew to love with silence.

Now there's a man shredded from the beginning, who can't find the balance between saying and not saying.

For days I keep how much I love you inside myself and you blame me for keeping quiet.

I don't know what's enough. In the bible a man begged for a drop of water to be placed on his tongue.

Burning with love, I looked at you and thought that was enough.

You turn and say I live too much inside myself, leaving you all alone outside.

In my dreams you have your head resting on my chest and are satisfied.

There are many rooms inside myself, find the one you're comfortable in;

shut the door behind you. I'm already inside.

FIRST GIRL VISIT: HIGH SCHOOL

The day before she visits, I turn over the mattress,
run my hand throughout to see if there are no spikes on this side.
The plan is to keep the curtains drawn in the kitchen tomorrow
to hide the huge hole in the window.
Nothing can be done about the coffee table with a broken side
which my younger brother calls a "convertible"
because of the top that comes off when he flips it over the couch every night
to make room to sleep.
Anyway, a man who hides everything is suspicious,
so I will let her see what cannot be hidden.
Tomorrow there'll be a smell of lavender on these tiles.

THE UNATTAINABLE

I stand staring at your lips in your small room,
thirsty for the wetness of your mouth.
You've said *No* about four times,
even when I asked for your forehead.
We've been doing this for some time whenever I'm in Cape Town—
going out for drinks, enjoying each other's company,
me wanting more, you drawing lines not to be crossed.
You ask me why I keep staring at you. I have no words.
I feel filthy. Unwanted.
In the car, I want to snatch my heart out
and only put it back when it has stopped aching.
But I will see you again.
Regardless.

THORNS IN MY HEART

Z has always been there. Always seeped through my relationships.
Always lingered.
I fell in love with her in primary school
with the innocence of a boy who hadn't seen much sin.
She rejected me with the innocence of a girl
who only knew her mother's love.
Years later she loves me with passion.
Years later I'm still trying to forgive her.
We love like shift workers.
I look for something more stable in between.
I don't know what she does.

S was four years older than me
and loved me with a mature heart
that had seen it all and knew what it wanted.
I loved her with the anxiety of what my parents would say,
what my friends would say.
People would think I was looking for a mother's love.
So I let her go.

T was looking for a home in me.
She found out I was a shack,
wrecked by the misfortunes of giving out a heart.
So she loved me with hope that she could rebuild me.
I loved her with a yearning to be mended.
Love felt like stitches and bandages.
But ruins won.

TH is a beautiful dream that vanishes when I wake up.

A fruit on a branch extending over a cliff.

The taste of my own medicine.

All of my past shortcomings having caught up with me.

ONE OF THE WAYS IN WHICH WE ENDED

Remembering S

You text to tell me you're finally at the taxi rank and can't wait
to see me. You must be smiling. I tell you not to catch the taxi.
I lie and say I'm very busy this weekend. But we both know
the truth- that a part of me that clings to loneliness has taken
charge. You call to say it's alright. And hang up immediately.
You've now mastered the tone that conceals pain. You don't
know how much that kills me. I want you to suffer with me
when I push you away. What sorcery is this anyway? Me stab-
bing you and being the one that dies? At night I toss and turn in
pain. My arm extending over your ghost lying next to me. In the
middle of the night I call to say *I'm sorry, so sorry.* You say *ok.*

SONG IN MY HEART

My girlfriend and I fight because I haven't yet mastered
the art of bathing in a dish.
Water spills all over the floor when I reach for my armpits.

She complains that I complain about this tiny room
where we hear kettles boil next door
and neighbours yawn as they wake up.

But I always return to drown our love-making with uKhozi FM.
It takes me three hours on a taxi to get to her.
The song in my heart keeps me company.

TO THE BUS STOP

It is drizzling. And I am walking next to a woman who drew our future
with her finger on my chest last night. She is holding a small umbrella
beneath which only she can fit. She has been calling me to join her, willing
to sacrifice half of herself to the wetness. I refuse. Just before we come to
the mall, a white Audi A3 lowers its speed to match ours. A young man in
the passenger seat holding a dumpy calls for her attention. He is asking to
talk to her. Asking for her number. Complimenting her legs. I stare at him
to reassure him that I exist. He keeps trying to talk to her unaffected by my
cold eyes. I keep my words inside me. I tell myself it will soon be over. He
gives up. The car speeds off and disappears around the corner. I point ahead
to the bus stop and tell my woman our bus has arrived.

THE WANDERING MAN

For T

My love poems always sound like obituaries,
always mourning someone that got away.
I told you this before you gave me your heart
but took care to not make it sound like a warning.
I am haunted by our memories:
Our long drives to beautiful landscapes
listening to James Bay;
my morning and late night drives
to and from you.
I am haunted by your thumb-sucking
like a 5-year-old.
I could have opened up my arms to shelter you forever,
but I'm a hopeless wandering man.
My heart is a hotel room up the stairs.
Lovers are always walking up and down
looking for a home.

ACKNOWLEDGMENTS

I am eternally grateful to Professor Kobus Moolman for his kindness and guidance.

Thanks to Dashen Naicker for his contribution to my writing, and also to Gary Cummiskey, the former editor of *New Coin.*

I would also like to express my gratitude to the editors of these publications in which earlier versions of the following poems appeared:

"The internal saboteur," "Absolution," and "I should pray" were published, with different titles, in *Agbowo.* Thank you once again Moyosore Orimoloye for reaching out and inviting me to send my work.

"Mother" appeared in the *2015 Sol Plaatje Poetry Anthology.*

"Absence" appeared as "Mother" in *Cutting Carrots the Wrong Way,* an anthology of prose and poetry on food by the University of the Western Cape postgraduate students in the Creative Writing Programme.